BORN

to BATTLE

By

PASTOR JOEY CASTLEBERRY

Copyright © 2013 by Pastor Joey Castleberry

Born to Battle
by Pastor Joey Castleberry

Printed in the United States of America

ISBN 9781628715323

Unless otherwise indicated, Bible quotations are taken from The King James Version of the Bible.

www.xulonpress.com

DEDICATION

This book is dedicated to all the men and women of God in my life who have helped me to get to where I am now. Your integrity, love, humility, and compassion for me and others have left an incredible impression on my life.

To all of my family...we have had our ups and downs, ins and outs, but when all was said and done, we were always there for each other.

To my children: Chelsie, Dalton, Dawson, and Jaycee...you're all definitely gifts from God. You bring me joy and happiness. Being your Daddy is a wonderful challenge and a great reward, and I am proud of each of you.

A special thanks to my mother, whose worth is immeasurable. I cannot thank you enough or begin to repay you for all that you have done for me.

To the people of LifeLion Ministries...your loyalty, support, and love are second to none. Your best and most blessed days lie ahead. I look forward to being a part of them.

To my wife, my best friend, thank you for all your love and labor to make our ministry and marriage work. Of all God's blessings upon me, you are one of the greatest.

But most of all, a fervent and most worshipful thank you to my Heavenly Father, who found this poor lost soul and gave him an anointing to lead a flock of His children. He blessed my tongue and lips to speak forth His truth, which is the Living Waters. May He bless this book so that it reaches the lost and leads them into His Kingdom.

FOREWORD

B*orn to battle*. That title means a whole lot to me, for I was truly born to battle. God has brought me through so much to put me here, able to put my struggles into words so that it may, in some way, bless others. It is my prayer that this book blesses you, the reader, and helps you to understand the love and the glory that is our God.

I searched the Bible for the best example I could find to illustrate someone who was born to battle. I found it in the book of Esther, which is an amazing book packed full of drama, power, romance, and intrigue. It shows the rise of an orphan girl from the pit to the palace, from scrubbing floors to giving orders.

Esther was born to battle. When the former queen refused to obey the king, she was banished from the kingdom. A decree was sent out to gather all the beautiful women in the empire together for a beauty pageant to let the king pick his new queen. Esther was one of the hand-picked contestants, and she found favor with the king.

Regardless of your station in life, if you obey and serve God, He will favor you. Just like Esther, you can rise from where you are. You may be as low as you have ever been, but you are not too far down that God cannot reach and elevate you.

There was a wicked politician named Haman that served under Esther's husband, the king, who wanted to kill all the Jews. Satan is always trying to steal, kill, and destroy the children of God. The problem that Haman had was that Esther was a Jew. Esther's uncle, Mordecai, found out about the plans and schemes of the enemy and told Esther.

"You have got to do something," Mordecai said to Esther, "all our people are going to perish if you don't do something."

Esther thought like you and I often have done, "Who am I? What can I do?" And, just like you and I, she had every excuse in the book.

Mordecai said to Esther once, "You were born for a time such as this." To paraphrase, "you were born to battle."

You and I were born to battle also. We were born to fight the things that are trying to kill our people. We were born to battle the hurts, habits, and hang-ups of our people. We were born to battle addictions, depression, and suicide on behalf of our lost loved ones. We were born to undermine the enemy's schemes and plans to tear down and destroy others and to help people fight their way to freedom.

I have good news: Esther saved the day, and so can you. The same thing God did through and for Esther, He will do through and for you. Rise up and fight for your people. You were born to battle. You are **somebody**, and you can make a difference. You can change the outcome. Help me fight the fight of faith because you were **born to battle**.

INTRODUCTION

Proverbs 21:31: *The horse is prepared for the day of battle: but deliverance is of the Lord.*

The white horse in this scripture is symbolic of physical power, self will, and the flesh. We, as human beings, have been taught for some time now that we need only rely on our own power, will, and desires. We often try to become better citizens without help from our Heavenly Father, mistakenly believing that the way to morality is through our own power. Multitudes of people today are trying to quit habits, addictions, and compulsive disorders by will power alone. Try as they may, no matter how many "new leaves they turn over", they will never live the quality of life for which they are destined without the help of an All-powerful God.

God has the power to deliver us from whatever it is we are going through. There is nothing too hard for Him. Jesus Christ has the authority and power to overcome any addiction or stronghold in our life. He is the Prince of Peace who will step on the battlefield of your mind, roll up the sleeves of His robe, and kick Satan's butt for you—if you will let Him. His name alone holds ultimate power to make this possible.

Names are more important than people realize. The Bible says that the name of *Jesus* is above every name and is capable of accomplishing any feat. *Crystal Meth* is the name of one of the most popular street drugs at the present time, but this name is not greater than the name *Jesus. Cancer* is the name of one of the most deadly physical infirmities known to the medical field, but it is not greater than the name of *Jesus.* Call on His name and let Him begin the healing process of your spirit. Many believe that Jesus came to bring peace, but he also came to bring war against Satan, his minions, and sin itself.

In heaven, there is a white uncut stallion waiting that has never been ridden. When Jesus returns to Earth for His Bride (the Church), He is going to be riding this white Arabian warhorse. This really is not necessary because He can move through the atmosphere without any help from anyone or anything. Yet, He will choose to ride the white warhorse. As mentioned above, the horse is a symbol of flesh. Jesus Christ, in one last statement to the Devil, is going to "ride hard and put up wet" the flesh (this white horse). The flesh consists of all our failures, setbacks, and sins. Jesus Christ will saddle and break the flesh in your life if you will surrender all to Him. Through Jesus, God is able to help you overcome and defeat every obstacle in your life, as He has done for me in the past and continues to do even today.

I lay no claims on the title of author. I wrote this book with the sole purpose of getting it into the hands of the hopeless, to give them hope. I pray it will encourage the discouraged and tell the people who are held by the handcuffs of sin that Jesus Christ has the key to unlock them. God has been too good to me for me to keep silent, so I must share the wisdom that I have learned through life experience and God's Word. Perhaps this book will go places that I cannot and be the voice of God for someone in trouble.

Chapter One

THE EARLY YEARS

I was born July 15, 1975 in Valdosta, Georgia, feet-first with the umbilical cord wrapped around my throat. Some people were born to fight. Some children have to fight to get here, having been dealt a bad hand before birth. I was one such child. I, like other children, did not deserve some of the obstacles and battles that I was to face during my young life.

Many times, spiritually and physically, things appear fine on the outside, but there is a problem rapidly advancing on the inside. When I reached nine months old, I was diagnosed with asthma. Some battles are not fought and won overnight, as my mother would soon learn. She had previously raised two healthy boys, but I had the most advanced stage of asthma known of at that time. I was called a *chronic asthmatic*. This meant I had to have constant monitoring to prevent medical complications.

I had frequent asthma attacks. One time my left lung collapsed, and I was allergic to many foods and environmental things that would trigger reactions, resulting in hospitalization. I have traumatic childhood memories of the fear of death gripping me as I struggled for my next breath.

Asthma limited me as a child, being a restrictor as to how far I could go in sports and physical education. I spent holidays and birthdays in the hospital. I was transported to hospitals better equipped to handle advanced cases. From the time I was nine months old until I was fifteen years old, my mother's life was not her own because she was tied to a child that needed almost constant care.

I had my last asthma attack at age fifteen. It was said that I just outgrew asthma, but I did not have the power in me to outgrow anything. God was my healer. I give Him all the credit for the end of my issues with asthma.

> Isaiah 53:5 says: *But he (Jesus) was wounded for our transgressions. He was bound for our iniquities: the chastisement of our peace was upon him, and with his stripes we are healed.*

Jesus paid for our healing when He allowed himself to be handcuffed to a whipping post and received the lashes upon His body. His flowing blood washed away all of our infirmities, but we must claim that healing and then believe it will be done.

1st Corinthians 12:9, 28 and 30 teaches about the gifts (plural) of healing. Some of the gifts God gave us are doctors, nurses, EMTs, surgeons and the wisdom of knowledge they possess. The medical field can treat and mend and administer, but God does the actual healing.

> James 5:14-15 says: *Is any sick among you? let him call for the elders of the church; and let them pray over him, anointing him with oil in the name of the Lord: and the prayer of faith shall save the sick, and the Lord shall raise him up; and if he have committed sins, they shall be forgiven him.*

If you are struggling with sickness, do not give up. God still heals today. God gave us wisdom to do what the medical field instructs and faith to believe it is in His hands. Once I was an unhealthy child, unable to run and play as freely as my peers, but now I work out five to six days a week, and that once sickly boy who could not walk across the yard without being out of breath, can now run for miles. To God be the Glory! He is Jehovah Rapha—our healer!

Seduced by Satanic Whisperings

> Psalms 129:1-2: *Many a time they have afflicted me from my youth. Let Israel now say- Many a time they have afflicted me from my youth: yet they have not prevailed against me.*

Psalms 129 plainly tells us Satan is afflicting the youth. The psalmist is so sure of this that he repeated himself in case we did not get it the first time.

St. John 10:10 says: that Satan comes to *steal, kill and destroy*. He will *steal* the future of your youth. He will *kill* the hopes and dreams of our children. He will *destroy* the plans and destiny of our kids if we sit back on a seat of "do nothing", and allow him to do it.

Demonic spirits are strategically sent from Satan as assigned assassins to stop the plan and call of God from maturing in a child. I remember the first time I felt a seducing demonic spirit. I was around eight years old. I was spending the day with my grandmother. Every day at noon we would take approximately an hour long nap. This one particular day was different. My grandmother had a bedroom with two full-sized beds separated by a nightstand; she was in one bed asleep and I was in the other bed, restless. All of a sudden out of nowhere, I was bombarded by pornographic images flashing through my mind. This was not something that I was imagining on my own. I could not turn it off. It was tormenting.

You might say that this occurred a bit early at age eight, but these types of thoughts are common for young boys, even if not usually quite that young. I understand that young boys reach an age when they get interested in the opposite sex, but not at eight years old. I had not been molested, had not been wrongly touched in any way. I had never seen pornographic books or movies; and at this time, television was pretty reserved in its programming.

My point is this: I had not been exposed to anything that could have so vividly put those thoughts in my mind. These thoughts were not just PG-13 or normal rated R. They consisted of XXX satanic seduction. When I was eight years old, a real demonic spirit of lust walked in the house and climbed in bed with me. The sad thing is that the grown-up in the house was asleep. If we are spiritually asleep, Satan will molest the spirit and seduce the mind of our youth.

This story should not shock us because God's Word tells us that Moses and Jesus were sought after by Satan at early ages. Satan even went so far as to manipulate the minds of the rulers to kill all the male babies in hopes of getting the ones with potential. Read Matthew Chapter Two to understand this.

If you are experiencing tormenting thoughts, be encouraged, there is help.

> Isaiah 9:6 says: *For unto us a child is born, unto us a son is given: and the government shall be upon his shoulder: and his name shall be called Wonderful, Counselor, The mighty God, The everlasting Father, The Prince of Peace.*

He is Jehovah…shalom. He is the Prince of Peace that can put an end to the torment.

I once heard a story that illustrated the battle of good and evil for our souls. An old Indian chief was mentoring a young warrior and told him a story of two wolves fighting on the inside of a man. One wolf was lust, hate, envy, greed, malice, murder (all of the negative aspects of humanity) and the other wolf was love, joy, peace, long-suffering, gentleness, goodness, and self-control (all of the positive aspects of humanity). The young warrior asked the life-seasoned chief which wolf won the fight. The chief's reply was "the one you feed the most wins."

Begin to read the Bible and feed your mind the Word of God and peace will flood your soul, allowing all of the positivity of God's love to lead you to a better you.

An Early Encounter with Rage

Webster says rage is a "violent and uncontrolled anger, a fit of violent wrath that goes unchecked."

Ephesians 4:26: *Be ye angry, and sin not...*

The emotion of anger is not a sin; what you do while you are angry can be a sin. Anger, channeled in the right way, can actually be helpful and beneficial. Sometimes people get angry with themselves because of a failure or something that went wrong. Anger will make you say, "Come Hell or high water, I'm not doing that again." In other words, anger can actually help you to learn from your mistakes, which can be a good thing.

I also had bad experiences with rage. One such episode occurred when I was somewhere between the ages of 9 and 10. My brother had a 1989 CJ7 Jeep Renegade that I used as a playhouse. I sat behind the steering wheel with the radio on, pretending to drive like any child might do. One day when I was in the Jeep, for some unknown reason, I got angry and the anger turned to violent feelings of rage. I began to beat the instrument panel of the Jeep. I was still small and frail due to health problems, but I took my fist and repeatedly beat the speedometer glass until it was in pieces. I cut my knuckles to the bone, but I still kept beating it. I ended up having to go get stitches.

Rage was a spirit that would often show up in my life. I could turn it on like a light switch, and I learned to use it to get what I wanted. We may play a physical temper tantrum game and get our way with people, but God does not play those games. He will not give you your way just because you pout or get mad, but He will bless you for your obedience to His Word.

St. Mark 5:1-20 records the story of a man that was demon-possessed. The townspeople tried to bind him up with chains and shackles, but the spirit of rage would engage and he would break the chains. He was so full of rage he was tormented and driven to cut himself with rocks. The people in town were afraid of him, but when Jesus showed up and "showed out", He cast the spirits out and set the man free.

2 Corinthians 3:17 says: *...where the spirit of the Lord is, there is liberty.*

Get in God's presence and He will liberate you.

The only way I can describe rage is that it is like a super-charged revved up engine that cannot be stopped. However, even the rankest spirit of rage must bow in the presence of Jesus. Read St. Mark Chapter 5. The demon-possessed man scared everyone else, but fell at Jesus' feet. Amen.

The Devastation of Divorce

In Genesis 2:18, God said: *It is not good that the man should be alone; I will make him a help meet for him.*

Recorded in verses 19-22 is a description of how God made man's helpmate. In verse 24, scripture says: *Therefore shall a man leave his father and mother, and shall cleave unto his wife: and they shall be one flesh.*

23

God took a rib out of Adam and made Eve. In Hebrew, the rib means "beam". When a man gets weak and bends under the load and pressure of stress, the woman is to stand behind him like a beam for strength and support. Satan undermines this purpose through separation and divorce.

When I was eight years old my mother and father divorced. Divorce is devastating to a child. The absence and abandonment of a parent is traumatic to the spirit of a child. I have overheard women say that they have had to be both mother and father. That is impossible. There are things instilled in children by a father that a mother just cannot give, and vice versa.

Many times, children feel rejected, let down, and like they are to blame for the divorce. They hear too many grown-up conversations concerning all the mess of a dysfunctional marriage. Through these adult conversations, that we are not careful to keep from our children's hearing, we put heavy burdens on their backs, and after divorce, when a child is abandoned, it opens up doors for lifelong problems...and for Satan's minions to step in and do their dastardly work.

Children can often be found lying to cover up the failures of a parent. On Career Days, when all the Dads are there telling about their great jobs, the abandoned child will fabricate a story of where his

Dad is and the reason for his Dad not being there. This child will often paint his Dad as a heroic figure, but the simple truth is he is not off being a hero; he is just not there because he is a zero.

Also, after divorce, parents use children as a weapon against an ex-spouse or in-laws because of bitterness and resentment. We have the power of life and death in our tongues, and often a parent will brainwash a child with negativity, bitter murmurings, and constantly reliving the past. Some children even feel pressured to hold back love and affection from one parent because the other parent will bring it up or make them feel bad or guilty.

God said he would be a father to the fatherless. There is hope and help and life on the other side of divorce. I refuse to let something I went through when I was eight years old control my life. My Mama and Daddy divorced each other, not me. Do not let divorce or its aftermath control you; love, honor, and respect your parents and trust God to bring healing.

Building the Battlement on the Roof

Deuteronomy 22:8: When thou buildest a new house, then thous shalt make a battlement for thy roof, that thou bring not blood upon thine house, if any man fell from thence.

In Israel the roofs are often built flat because people spend a lot of time on the roof. Families there cook, eat, party, watch festivals and have many social gatherings on the roof. The battlement Moses was talking about building is a handrail around the perimeter of the roof for safety. He was warning the people to build a handrail on the roof to keep kids from falling off, warning them to build a safe house for their children, instructing them to build a safe haven so their children would grow up free from being destroyed in their own home.

God still uses this scripture to instruct us to build a safe home, free of domestic violence, pornography, alcohol and drugs. When we bring sin into our homes, our children are more likely to fall. We need to build a battlement around our homes. We need to monitor what our kids listen to, watch on television, and view on the computer. We also need to monitor who we so freely invite into our homes.

One example of how not monitoring who is brought into our homes can cause negative experiences in a child's life happened to me. I lost my virginity when I was around 10 years old to someone who was viewed as harmless and was allowed into our home. The girl was in her early teens, and we were left alone for several hours. The Devil did his handiwork because of my parents' laxness.

Do not give Satan a doorway into your home. Do not leave your kids alone and unattended. Thousands of children are molested and fondled every year because the battlement has not been built in their home. When a child finds pornography in the home, it opens the floodgates for the enemy to come in and pervert their mind. So do not just childproof your home by locking up dangerous items; remove them completely. Build a safe house. If you have experienced a fall in your own home, there is hope. God will heal your hurts, allow you to forgive and move on. Many people are living with hate because of being hurt in their own home. Tell God where you hurt, ask Him to help you, and believe that He will do so.

Being Taught Wrongly for So Long

The Bible says the power of life and death is in the tongue. A child's mind is like a sponge, soaking up everything they hear. I acquired what I like to call "stinking thinking" by listening to front porch and dinner table talks from grown-ups who were just plain wrong in their viewpoints.

People are not born racist, they learn it from what they hear and are taught by the tongue of a person full of hate. People are not born hating homosexuals. God hates the sin of homosexuality, not the person who is homosexual. We are to hate the act, but love the person and try to show them the way to a Godly life. Children are taught by the tongues of wrong people to be homophobic. Children are not born with a vocabulary of profanity; it is programmed by the tongues of the people they are around. Many children are taught to believe in superstitions which can lead to demonic bondage through witchcraft. We tell our children silly things like "if you break a mirror, you will have seven years bad luck" and "walking under a ladder is bad luck". I was taught that if a black cat crossed the road, you could make an *X* mark on the windshield and cancel out the bad luck that the cat would bring.

If you are saved by the cleansing blood of Jesus Christ, a broken mirror, walking under a ladder, or a black cat, or any other silly superstition or spell cannot determine the outcome of your day. God's

Kingdom is not governed by luck. It is governed by the principles and precepts of the Bible.

As you begin to read God's Word, which is a spiritual mirror, it will allow you to see yourself as you really are. When you look in the mirror and see your hair is out of place, you comb it. Likewise, when you read the Bible and you see your life is out of place, ask God for help to fix it. The rules for using God's Word are this simple: Follow His Word and you will be blessed. Do not follow it, and you will be cursed. Let us begin to speak words of life and love over our kids and grandkids so they will not have a battle with "stinking thinking".

Chapter Two

THE PRESSURE OF PEERS AND TEENAGE YEARS

C hildren today have so many distractions—things that are designed to sidetrack them. The pressure to be accepted or to fit in is a major distraction. Satan has set so many traps through peer pressure.

As I look back over my life, I recall many times when people would pressure other people to drink or do drugs and use seduction to pressure people to satisfy sexual desires. I was addicted to alcohol, nicotine, and sex, and I acquired a taste for these between the ages of 13-16. I started dipping smokeless tobacco when I was 15 years old. The first dip placed in my mouth got me high. It may have seemed harmless to the adult that gave it to me, but they also handed me a one-can-a-day addiction. It was a pricey addiction too, at almost five dollars a can at today's prices.

It is amazing how we overlook the warning labels. It plainly says "May cause gum disease, tooth loss, and mouth cancer", yet we ignore those warnings in order to satisfy our habits. Mouth cancer is not cool. Do not give in to the pressure to use tobacco.

God's Word is a warning label, yet thousands of people die every year from nicotine addiction. If you smoke or chew tobacco, ask God for help. He is a deliverer. There will not be any spittoons or smoking areas in Heaven.

There is a term called "guilty by association". If you are in the vehicle with someone that commits a crime, you are just as guilty as they are, by law. Do not be guilty of allowing your kids to stay with or hang around people who are going to be a negative influence. Do not be guilty of allowing your kids to stay with people who will pressure them to use tobacco, to drink, or to use drugs. If you have been a stumbling block to someone or if you have introduced someone to a controlled substance such as nicotine, alcohol, or drugs, ask God to forgive you. The Bible says in Psalms 103:12 that He will cast your sins … *as far as the east is from the west.*

Babies Having Babies

Young people all across the world are having under-aged sex, premarital sex, and adding insult to injury, they are having babies in the process. It is sad to see a teenage girl who has not had the opportunity to be a normal child because she has a baby on her hip. It is sad to see a young man putting college on hold to work a minimum wage job, just to be able to buy diapers. There is nothing wrong with a minimum wage job. It is just that so many young men and women are pressured into a low-paying job for which they have to settle because of an under-aged pregnancy.

It should break our hearts to see young girls that cannot cook or clean house, wash clothes or iron. Many of these girls will not even work, choosing instead to look for government bailouts. Yet we wonder what is wrong with the economy today.

It should break our hearts to see young men, many of which sit up all night still playing video games, dressing like thugs and punks, trying to raise a generation just like them.

In 1st Corinthians 13:11, the Apostle Paul said: *When I was a child, I spake as a child, I understood as a child, I thought as a child: but when I became a man, I put away childish things.*

Let us put away childish things and become men and women of God.

I was party to an under-aged pregnancy at the age of 16. The mother of my kids was 15. I should have been at the house studying. I should have been home cleaning my room. Instead, I was parked under a river bridge, in a place I should not have been, doing something I should not have been doing. Guess what? Nine months later, "Whoop der she is." She was my oldest daughter.

When the mother of my children told me she was pregnant, I was gripped with great fear, shame, embarrassment and many other unmentionable emotions. I was not an attendant of any church at the time and my first reply to her was to get an abortion. I thank God she did not do that because we would not have had our daughter Chelsie, who was a model child and student, homecoming queen, honor graduate, and a college graduate.

If you have had an abortion in the past, stop tormenting yourself with regrets, ask God to forgive you and move on with your life. If you continue to play the "shoulda, coulda, wouldas" over in your mind, it will only destroy you. God forgives and gives life. If you are a young couple, or a young single parent with a child, you need God on your side to help you successfully raise your children.

Life is full of choices and consequences. Our choices have consequences and repercussions. I had a choice to have sex or not, I did have sex and it had a consequence. Many people get mad at God concerning the way their life turned out. The book of Proverbs says that people ruin their lives by their own foolish mistakes, then get mad and blame God.

I was no different in this aspect; I made my own wrong choices and had to deal with them. I went to work, not to buy clothes for me, but to buy diapers for my baby. My life changed because of my wrong choices.

Seek God for guidance; make good choices. God can make your rocky road smooth and your crooked road straight. God is not the one to blame. God is our help, not our hindrance. Stop blaming everyone else and face the facts that we just make terrible choices sometimes. Repent and move on. Our God will help you through your problems even if they are self-induced. Many things we view as a problem at the moment, we realize down the road are our greatest blessings.

Victims of Violence

Psalms 11:5: *The LORD trieth the righteous: but the wicked and him that loveth violence his soul hateth.*

It is getting more and more common to read or hear about child or teenage violence. It is hard to imagine a child killing another child, and it is hard to understand how a teenager can kill someone for no apparent reason, with no motive in mind. Since it is hard to understand how something works unless you have worked it, I have a pretty good understanding about violence. I have participated in an aggravated assault, several cases of battery and have been charged with three felonies. The violence did not just appear when I was an adult; it was instilled and transferred to me when I was a child.

Children who witness their mama being beaten often grow up and beat their spouses. There are cases that this is not true, however. It is like the story of two brothers who has a dad who is an alcoholic. One brother grew up to be an alcoholic and the other one became a teetotaler. When someone asked the alcoholic brother why he chose to drink, he said "because my Daddy was a drunk." When they asked the brother who lived a life of sobriety why he chose not to drink, his reply was "my Daddy was a drunk." There is no excuse for violence or to put your hands on your spouse in a harming way.

I saw my dad beat my mom. I heard them cuss and fuss and argue. There is an old saying "the apple never falls far from the tree." I was 17 and had a child that witnessed me cussing at and beating her mama. Although you cannot change the fact that "the apple never falls far from the tree", what you can change is the kind of fruit the tree produces.

> The Bible says in Galatians 5:22: … *the fruit of the spirit is love, joy, peace, long-suffering, gentleness, goodness, faith, meekness, temperance: against such there is no law.*

If we will give our lives to God, fill our spirit with God, our attitudes and mindsets will change and our behavior will change. The fruit that falls from a good tree will produce good fruit.

> In Proverbs 23:7, the Bible states: …*for as he (a man) thinketh in his heart: so is he…*

When a child fills his or her mind with video game violence, television violence, or when they witness firsthand domestic violence, the chances of their becoming violent are very likely. Where the mind goes the man usually follows. If a man's mind is in the gutter, he usually ends up there. Let us fill our minds with God's Word, so we can follow Him.

Chapter Three

THE BEGINNING OF ALCOHOLISM

Proverbs 20:1: *Wine is a mocker, strong drink is raging: and whosoever is deceived thereby is not wise.*

I remember when I was 14 years old, and I got hold of a bottle of cooking wine. That was one of the worst mistakes I ever made, and it was the worst stomach ache I ever had. However, the pain soon wore off, as most pains and punishments do, and it was not severe enough to stop me from repeating my mistake of drinking alcohol. The reason people continue to get in trouble is that the punishment often does not outweigh the pleasure.

Speaking of punishment and sins, or crimes, there is a very valid point I wish to make. Scriptures concerning judgment of our sins are often misunderstood. For instance, the Old Testament scripture that says "an eye for an eye and a tooth for a tooth" was never meant for personal revenge. It was a law given to judges telling them that the punishment should fit the crime. It was, in laymen's terms, telling them not to slap a bank robber on the hand and imprison a jaywalker.

Now, let us get back to my first experience with drinking. The pain and memory of how sick I got from the cooking wine incident soon left me, not forgotten, but also not so vivid in my mind, at least not vivid enough to keep me from drinking again. At the age of 15, I found myself sitting on the front porch with one of my uncles. He said to me, "Joey go get me a beer out of the refrigerator and get you one if you want to. Just don't tell your Mama."

I did as he asked. I had a beer with him. It was a 12-ounce Budweiser in the can, and it was the first of thousands. As I said, I was 15, and I am 38 at the writing of this book, and I still remember popping the top, the sound of the opening of the can, the cold steam rolling out of the can, and the taste. I took two swallows and it was gone. My eyes watered, my lips got numb. I was hooked. I had my drink of choice. Like most alcoholics I would drink anything, but if I was buying, my choice was Budweiser.

I started drinking every chance I got. When I was in high school, I would drink a 12-pack on Friday and Saturday nights. And when I turned 21, I would drink a 12-pack a day and a case on Friday, Saturday, and Sunday. I drank everywhere I went. I remember that when I went to visit someone in the hospital, I usually stopped by the store and got a cup, lid, and a straw and carried beer with me through the hospital. I had a cooler by my bed full of beer.

I went on a four-year binge. I would drink so much my body could not pass it through urination and I would vomit, not because I was sick, but because I had so much alcohol in my system. After I vomited and made room for more alcohol in my stomach, I would go right back to drinking.

Alcohol is an addiction that destroys lives and shatters dreams. People turn to the bottle trying to cope with life's problems and end up with a greater problem than they had.

The Bible says God created the Garden of Eden, and He created Adam and Eve. He put two trees in Eden, the Tree of Knowledge of Good and Evil and the Tree of Life which He told Adam and Eve not to touch. Eve ate the fruit of the Tree of Knowledge of Good and Evil, and she gave some to Adam and he ate. Immediately they knew they were naked. They saw themselves in a way they were never intended to see each other, and the Bible said that they hid themselves.

When you indulge in things you were never intended to touch, you see things in a way you were never intended to see them. That is why some men get drunk and see a 10 year old girl as a 30 year old woman and cross the line, destroying a life through molestation. Some men get drunk and see their wives as punching bags. Some people get intoxicated and see other people's things as their own and take them.

Beer ads look good, everyone smiling, everyone having a good time. The picture they do not paint is the dead bodies in a ditch after a tragic wreck. Satan is very good at making the wrong things look so right and enticing, and we fall for that illusion more times than not, and then proceed to destroy our lives and those of our loved ones by becoming drunks.

My alcoholism lasted from the time I was 15 until I was 27. I know some groups and people say that once you are an alcoholic, you are always an alcoholic. I know some people go to groups and stand up and say, "Hi, my name is Joey, and I am an alcoholic," and he may not have drunk a drop in 20 years. The Bible says when you get saved that you become a new creation and that the old things are passed away. The apostle Paul says to put away those things that are behind you and reach ahead to those things that are before you. Salvation cleanses you of your sins and the labels of association. I'm a blood-bought, tongue-talking, pew-running, Holy Ghost-dancing, born-again child of God. Hi, my name is Joey, and I am **not** an alcoholic.

John 8:36 says: *If the son therefore shall make you free, ye shall be free indeed.*

Do not be deceived or let people lie to you.

The Word of God says in 1st Corinthians 6:10: *No drunkard shall inherit the kingdom of God.*

That is plain and simple. If you are struggling with an addiction of alcohol, do not give up. There is help. His name is Jesus.

Alcohol controls the minds of men. Many men think they are tough, but they are letting a 4-inch can whip them day in and day out. A lot of people drink to escape from reality. They drink to hide the way things really are behind a buzz, but the sad truth is every day you wake up with a headache a day older and with a stronger problem. Call on God. He is your help. Ask Him for His cleansing help and kick the habit. Sobriety is a precious thing.

I got saved when I was 27. I did not quit drinking "cold turkey". You can call it "slow chicken" instead, but nevertheless, with God's help, after about three months of church attendance and prayer, we (God and I) kicked the habit. I like to be in control of my own thoughts, not controlled by a substance called spirits, and I am truly grateful to my Heavenly Father for making me sober.

Your sobriety is in your dedication to God.

1st Peter 5:8 says: *Be sober, be vigilant because your adversary the devil as a roaring lion walketh about seeking who he may devour.*

Do not let the enemy devour you through an alcohol addiction, when the power of God is so available. The hopes and dreams and lives of many children have been crushed by parents that could not control the demon of alcoholism in a battle.

Prevailing Over Pornography

Psalms 101:3: *I will set no wicked thing before mine eyes.*

When I was around the age of 12 or 13, I was in a particular house, and I was there alone. I got up, went to a bedroom, and stood in front of the chest of drawers. I went to the third drawer, opened it, moved some garments, and there it was…a VHS tape. I took the tape to the living room, put it in, and there was another new vice…hardcore XXX porn.

The Bible says Jesus was led by the spirit to the wilderness. I was led by a spirit that day, but it sure was not the Holy Spirit. I had never plundered through people's things and had not known that the VHS tape of porn was there. This incident had been a spiritual setup by Satan.

In 1st John 2:16, the Bible says: …*the lust of the eye is not of the father…it is of the world and the world will pass away.*

To pass away means to die. Lust is beatable, through God.

Gratefully, I was never addicted to porn. Like most young men if it was around I would look at it, but I was never addicted or controlled by it. When I was a child, I would find an occasional playboy book here and there, but this generation today has a major struggle with the lust of the eye. Pornography is everywhere. The internet makes so many things available. The sad fact is that sex sells; that is why on commercials or ads, you see these seductively dressed, mostly undressed, young ladies and men.

In the Bible, in Joshua chapter two, Joshua sent two spies to Jericho to look over the land. God was giving the town to Joshua and the children of Israel. When the spies got there, they stayed in the house of Rahab in Zoonah (which means *harlot* in Greek). She was a prostitute (*porne* in Greek); thus, any way you spell it, Rahab was a whore.

Joshua's spies stayed in a house full of porn and prostitution and did not sin. They displayed Godly character and Christian integrity. They were not blind, and they saw Rahab's beauty. It would have been easy for them to slip between the sheets of sin and feed their flesh there that night, but they were on a mission for God. Rahab had finally met some men that looked at her heart, not her body. She had finally met some men she could trust. She had finally met some men that came to give, not to get. They gave her something she had never had...love. She had had a bunch of sex, she had just never been loved. Because they loved her for who she was and not what she did, it so changed her that she wanted what they had (God).

This book is designed for you to study these scriptures as we go. I am not going to tell the whole story. Read it for yourself. But I will tell you that out of a whole city the only people that were spared were Rahab and her family. God delivered a prostitute and gave her hope and a new home. God saved a common street-whore and gave her a destiny. She later became the grandmother of King David.

It does not matter where you start out in life; it only matters where you end up. God has delivering power to cause you to turn your head from sin and porn. So many women go to bed lonely because their men are having affairs and/or are fantasizing about relationships with other women. These men are so enamored with the fantasy that they ignore the flesh-and-blood women who love them and who want to share themselves with them.

To be addicted or habitual is to be a person with a habit so strong that you cannot easily give it up. God never said it would be easy, He just said that you could do it. He never said the load could not get heavy, He said he would help you bear your burden. Do not low-rate and down-grade yourself by looking at porn. God made you to be better than that.

The reason that pornography and prostitution are wrong is that you cannot sell something that is not yours.

> 1st Corinthians 6:19 says: *Know ye not that your body is the temple of the Holy Ghost which is in you.*

God designed your body to be the temple (church), not a trash can for the filth of the world. Rise up men and women of God and overcome porn and perversion. Fill your mind with the Word of God.

> Proverbs 16:3 says: *Commit your works unto the Lord and your thoughts shall be established.*

If you commit and dedicate yourself to God, He will change your mind and thoughts.

Lottery or Gambling

Proverbs 28:22 says: *He that hasteth to be rich hath an evil eye, and considereth not that poverty shall come upon him.*

I do not play the lottery. I pay tithes. I do not throw my money away on a one-in-a-million chance. I put my money in a sure thing—God's Kingdom.

King David said, "I was once young and now I am old, and I have never seen the righteous forsaken and their seed begging bread."

Some children do without school clothes because of a gambling habit of a parent. Give God His portion, and watch Him bless your life.

As mentioned earlier in this book, in the Garden of Eden, God placed two trees, the Tree of Knowledge of Good and Evil and the Tree of Life. God told Adam and Eve not to eat of them. God was letting them know that those trees were His portion. When they ate God's portion, it cursed the ground and caused sin to enter their home.

God's portion is called *tithes*. According to the Bible, it is 10 percent of your income. To learn more about tithes, read the book of Malachi, which explains it best.

Chapter Four

WITCHCRAFT, SPELLS, GHOSTS & SUPERSTITIONS

Exodus 22:10: *Suffer not a witch to live.*

Witchcraft gives honor to the devil. The Bible says that we are to worship God, the Father, the Son, and the Holy Spirit alone. In the Old Testament they were instructed to kill witches, but it did not always happen that way. King Saul signed a decree to have all witches killed. Later, he inquired of the Witch of Endor. It is not ironic that Samantha's mother in the TV series *Bewitched* is named *Endora*?

When Jesus came, God wrapped in a flesh suit, the Bible was made flesh. He tore the veil, and the world embraced Grace and Mercy in the fullest. We now live in the Dispensation of Grace. God forbids the physical killing of people now, unless it is instituted by the judicial court. However, as Christians, we are to engage in a spiritual battle against the principalities, powers and rulers of darkness, witches, spells and warlocks and to kill their evil desires. We kill the evil desires of the dark world through prayer, fasting, praise and worship.

This generation is so enthused by the paranormal. There are many major box office hits focused on paranormal activity. Numerous television shows (tell-a-vision) that deal with witches, mediums, psychics, and paranormal activity.

Witches, warlocks, and spells do not concern me as much as the people that do not believe that they exist or that they have power.

My grandmother who died in 1994 at the age of 78 lived in Jasper, Florida when she was 13 years old, and there was a fortune teller set up on the street where she lived. This psychic, or witch, told my grandmother that she was going to have a hard life, a life of poverty and pain. My grandmother accepted and believed that negative and false prophecy from Hell and lived it out. The Bible tells us that we can have life, health and wealth. Do not let seeds of negative speech grow in you. Some people are told they are no good, and that they will never amount to anything. Some young girls are beaten down by the negative tongue of a man that wants to control them.

There is no spell or negative word that the blood of Jesus Christ cannot cancel out.

My grandmother loved me, and I loved her. She was very much like me. She was a tough woman. She had a lot of nerve, and she would fight at the drop of a hat and was often the one to drop the hat. In her elder years, she was diagnosed with dementia, and later Alzheimer's, and lived miserably for years in a nursing home. She died when I was 20 years old, but the negative spirit within her still lived.

When a person dies the spirits that negatively influenced or troubled them do not die. Instead, they seek a new home.

I had never been to church much while growing up, and I did not know anything about witchcraft or the occult. I was standing in the funeral home at the casket, overlooking my grandmother's lifeless body. As clear as a bell, I heard a demonic spirit tell me to take a lock of her hair. I reached in my pocket, pulled out a yellow-handled double X pocket knife and cut a lock of my grandmother's hair and placed it in my wallet. Immediately, I entered into a covenant with the demonic spirit that had such a negative effect on my grandmother. As a result, I was tormented for seven years by a spirit of anger and rage.

It amazes me at the people who do not believe that demons exist, including many preachers.

> In Ephesians 6:12, Paul said: ...*we wrestle not against flesh and blood, but against principalities, against powers, against the rulers of the darkness of this world, against spiritual wickedness in high places.*

He was speaking of demons. We battle demons in the spiritual realm, which affects us in the physical realm.

I experienced demonic influence for seven years; this demonic spirit would enrage me, which led to my going through a revolving door of jail incarceration because I loved to fight.

I was in Lowndes county jail in 2003, an alcoholic, bound by lust, anger, addicted to nicotine, adrenaline, controlled by rage and a demonic spirit that had had his eyes on me for years, just waiting on the right time to set up camp in my spirit. I cried out to God for help, He saved my soul, covered my heart and mind with the blood of Jesus and cancelled out all the plans of the enemy.

James 2:19 says: *Thou doest well, the devils also believe and tremble.*

When I cried out to God, Jesus Christ walked into Lowndes County Jail spiritually, kicked open my cell, saved my soul, rolled up the sleeves of his robe and beat that demon all up and down 120 Prison Farm Rd. God is great and greatly to be praised. There is nothing too hard for God. The Bible says God kicked Satan out of Heaven on a lightning bolt. He whipped Satan faster than the speed of light. There is lightening in his fist and thunder in his footsteps. Call Him for help and he will help you conquer and overcome.

There is a great amount of talk about ghosts. There are television shows centered on ghosts... friendly ghosts, long-lost loves that come back to comfort the living. The disciples even mention the word "ghost". Jesus came walking on water and they perceived it to be a ghost. We now have ghost busters, ghost hunters, and ghost monitors.

The Bible records a story where a rich man dies, and from Hell he opens his eyes and sees Lazarus in Abraham's bosom. He tells Abraham to send Lazarus with some water. Abraham tells him of a great gulf; he says Lazarus cannot come back.

While you are alive, you have a choice where you will spend eternity. God said "I put before you two paths: one to life (Heaven), one to death (Hell). Choose which one you want." Obey God and you will spend eternity in Heaven; disobey God and you will spend eternity in Hell. It is that simple. After you die, you either go to Heaven or Hell. You do not get to wander around here on earth, so ghosts do not really exist.

> The Bible says in Hebrews 9:27: *And as it is appointed unto men once to die, but after this the judgment:*

I have heard dying people tell loved ones that they will always be here. I am sorry, but that is not so. The Bible says that Satan can appear as an Angel of Light, and if you have seen something that you call a ghost, you have either seen an angel or a demon. I assure you that you have not seen a person that just wants to wander around the earth after dying.

God is in control and His Word is true. God created Heaven for the people who accept Jesus Christ as their personal savior to live for eternity in peace, and God created Hell for Satan and his army of demons and imps, and for all those who deny Christ.

Do not waste your time on ghost stories. Serve God and let the Holy Ghost lead you to all truths.

We are all familiar with superstitions especially in the South. People are taught to be afraid to walk under a ladder. Some people have broken mirrors and feared seven years of bad luck. As children, we would skip down the sidewalk dodging cracks for fear of breaking our mothers' backs. Some people believe if a black cat crosses the road you can put an *X* on the windshield and cancel out any bad luck. Some people believe it is bad luck to close a pocket knife somebody else opened, and the list of silly superstitions goes on and on.

You are not governed by Lady Luck. The Bible says in Deuteronomy Chapter 28 that if you obey God you will be blessed. If you disobey God you will be cursed. I have too much invested in God, and He has too much invested in me, to let a cat take my blessing and give me a bad day. I have prayed too many prayers to let a broken mirror cause me to have misfortune. My blessings come from God, not chance or happenstance.

Do not believe the deception of a horoscope. I called it *horroscope*. *Horror* means to be fearful and *scope* means to see clearly.

God said in 2nd Timothy 1:7: *He did not give us the spirit of fear but power and of love and a sound mind.*

Do not believe fortune cookies or horoscopes. Put your trust in God. I will trust His judgment over that of a newspaper horoscope any day.

In the town where I was raised, there were certain people that were believed to have power to heal. One person would "talk warts off people". Children with embarrassing warts would go to have them "talked off". My oldest daughter Chelsie and my son Dalton had a condition in their mouth, called thrash, which is common in children. It is a white powdery substance that appears on their tongue and the roof of their mouth. I took my children to a person who I was told could cure the thrash. The person took my children into a private room, without me, and chanted something over them, and the thrash went away. I am sure others have done the same. We were all wrong in doing so. We opened doors in our children's lives to the dark spiritual realm when we did this.

I want to bring some biblical clarity to all this, anything that is done outside of Jehovah God and without the name *Jesus* is witchcraft and of the devil. You may be thinking that Satan does not do good acts, and he will not heal. You may be thinking if a child was cured of an illness, how it could be that witchcraft can heal him.

2nd Corinthians 11:14 says: *And no marvel* (don't think it strange) *for Satan himself is transformed into an angel of light.*

Satan will do minor acts of goodness to get you further into bondage, to result in greater destruction in the end. He (Satan) can appear as an angel of light, making it appear as if he is doing you a favor. He appears to be giving you a helping hand, but his motive is destruction. He tricks us into thinking it is all harmless, convincing us to participate in our own destruction. People call psychic hotlines for a glimpse of their future, and they open a door in the spirit realm for demonic activity. Children play with Ouija boards, which are gateways for demonic access into their lives.

The Bible tells us that our healing was paid for by the stripes that Jesus bore on his back, and that there is no name other than *Jesus* by which men can be saved. Satan does not and cannot truly heal us. This is only a deceptive means to fill us with his evil.

When I accepted Jesus as my personal savior, and the knowledge of the truth was made plain through His Word, I anointed my children with oil and denounced the working of Satan off their life. You should do the same.

> In Matthew 28:18 Jesus says: ...*All power is given unto me in heaven and in earth.*

When Jesus gave his life on the cross, he defeated death, Hell, and the grave. The acceptance of the blood of the last sacrificial lamb can and will cancel out any spell, any curse, any superstition of the enemy. It will free you of gambling addictions too. Ask Jesus into your heart and evict the plans of Satan.

Chapter Five

PILL MY PAIN

Revelation 21:4: *And God shall wipe away all tears from their eyes; and there shall be no more death, neither sorrow, nor crying, neither shall there be any more pain...*

P ain is a terrible thing. Webster says that pain is a bodily sensation marked by discomfort, punishment, and distress. There are so many ways and areas in which to experience pain. There are so many places in our being that can hurt. Whether it is minor or major, no one likes pain. There is physical pain, emotional pain, psychological pain and many more kinds of pain.

Some people are living with the pain of losing a loved one, while others are living with the pain of all their personal failures. Some people have physical pains caused by car wrecks, falls, mishaps and accidents. Still other people have the pain of a crushed spirit and a broken heart. Nevertheless pain is pain and the truth is that nobody likes it, nobody wants it, and it really hurts. Everyone is looking for some way to ease their pain. This pain pill craze has gotten out of hand because of people seeking quick, easy pain relief, causing so many people to become addicted to pain pills. This addiction is rampant. People take a pill to get them up in the morning, a pill to keep them going at noon, and a pill to put them to sleep at night. Today, there are pills for everything.

Sometimes we create problems trying to cope with things that become greater than the initial problem we had. We should pray when we get stressed out, instead of taking the pills the medical field is handing out. God will help us with our stress and pain if we will only ask. One of His names is *Jehovah Rophi*, which means *God Who Heals*; thus, He is our healer. Instead, when people are hurting, our society just pills their pain. Some doctors are no better than street drug lords and dealers, just handing out pain pills to people that do not really need them.

Hosea chapter 4 says that people sacrifice with harlots (play with harlots) and that the people that "doth not understand shall fall." (Verse 14) Read it for yourself.

God said, "My people play with too many har-lots." Is it not ironic that most street drugs and pills have nicknames that are women's names? *Lori*-tab, *Crystal*-meth, *Mary-Jane*, *Roxi*, *Molly*, *Angel* dust. A pain pill does not fix the problem. It just numbs us to reality. When people hate the way their life is going and cannot stand to look reality in the eyes, they pill their pain and escape to a fantasy world that does not exist.

When I used to drink, I drank to numb an internal pain. Getting drunk and/or doped up is a coward's way out. A real man, or a real woman, will soberly face the truth and ask God to help them change the way it is.

My daddy was a dreamer. He had good inten-tions, but he would listen to the demon in a bottle of whiskey and hide the truth behind a buzz, and drown responsibility behind the pain of a hangover. I am not anti-medicine. I am a realist. I know some people hurt beyond comprehension and that some people need pain killers, but, for the most part, people are addicted, have a habit, and the pain is long gone.

Did you know that they tried to give Jesus a pain killer? When He was on the cross, they had a bucket of pain killer, which was vinegar mixed with gall. It was all they had in that time. They put a rag on a long pole, soaked it in pain killer, and lifted it to His lips. When He tasted it, He spit it out. By Him doing that, His statement echoed the words, "I choose to be sober and free." When He refused to numb His pain, He conquered the spirit of addiction and you can too.

Pain pills are being passed around like Satan's candy. People who do not even have problems go to doctors to get pills, leaving medical debts that are paid for by taxpayers, and then they wonder why the economy is in trouble.

The Bible says, "But seek ye first the Kingdom of God." Go to God before you go to the medicine cabinet. He is still a healer. He is still a comforter. God has the power to help you overcome your addictions and habits. If you have a family member or friend addicted to pills, do not give up on them. Keep praying and keep loving them. God can deliver you or them.

Some people are trying to physically medicate a spiritual problem. Ask God for help. He is waiting and listening for you.

In Psalms 25:18, David said: *Look upon mine affliction and my pain...*

God knows where you hurt, He sees and He is waiting for you to make an appointment. Let us pray for our deliverance from pill addictions.

Chapter Six

OUTGROWING RACISM

Acts 10:34: *Then Peter opened his mouth, and said, Of a truth I perceive that God is no respecter of persons:* (In layman's terms, God is not prejudiced nor does He bless racism.)

I was raised and taught to be a racist. I was told early in life that people of other colors and races were beneath us, not to an extreme, but it was enough to cause bondage. I never really bought into the lie of racism. I always saw people as people, and when I got saved, God began to reveal to me his biblical truth concerning racism.

If you claim to be a Christian and declare Heaven to be your next home, and you have hate in you for another race or hate a social group of people, you have a sad wake-up call coming. There are no seg-regated water fountains in Heaven for each separate race of people. On the bus going to Heaven, you get to sit in any seat you want. There are no back doors for lower races to knock on in Heaven. We will all be equal, and to get there you must view people as being equal on earth.

The Bible says that God created Adam out of the dust of the earth. Adam was a dirt bag. (Ha! Ha!) Laughter does a heart good. Amen. There is a color of dirt on earth for every skin color on people. There is white dirt for white people, black dirt for black people, brown dirt for Hispanics, red dirt for Native Americans, and so forth.

I have never owned a slave, and will not ever do so. I have never contributed to the physical slavery of any man and, having written that, I do not owe any man anything for them being in slavery. The Bible says, "Owe no man but to love him." It also says that we were born into sin (slavery).

> Jesus says in John 8:34: ...*Whosoever committeth sin is the servant of sin.*

He was saying that sin makes slaves of us. I was born in sin and lived as a slave to sin for 27 years of my life. Then I called on God and He broke my handcuffs, severed my shackles, and took the whip out of Satan's hand. He healed my back where Satan had plowed it with sin and selfishness.

In Acts 13:10, it records a story of Peter. He goes to sleep and has a dream. In his dream, he saw Heaven open up and a certain vessel descending to him. In this vessel was all manner of beasts: wild beasts, fowl of the air, and creeping things. There came a voice to Peter that said, "Rise, kill, and eat," but Peter said, "No, not so Lord, for I have never eaten anything unclean or common." The voice said, "What I have cleansed do not call common." This happened three times.

Peter was Jewish, and the animals in the vessel were symbolic of the Gentiles. Peter did not want to preach to the Gentiles; he thought he was better than they were. However, God told Peter to outgrow the racism. For Peter to move to the next level of anointing, he had to outgrow his old bigoted thought patterns.

I have heard people profess to be Christians, yet in general conversation they would use racial hate words. You know what these words are. Do not get all spiritual on me now. Some people are called *niggers*, some are called *wetbacks*, and some are called *crackers*. All of these words are wrong, and they are sinful for whoever uses them.

God looks at and examines the heart, not the color of our skin. If I need blood, a person of any other race's blood will work in my body as long as the type matches. Jesus died for every race, every color. The Bible says all that call "on the name of the Lord shall be saved." There are all kinds of organizations that are secret brotherhoods, and they often exclude other races from joining in at their meetings. There was a group formed in the Bible; it is called *the Church*, and all people of every color are welcome. God wants a multi-colored, multi-racial, multi-cultural church. If you cannot worship with a brother of another color here on earth, you surely will not worship with them in eternity. Call on God to destroy the root of racism in your heart.

White people are always building and have building programs going. Black people have got the praise. Hispanics are hard workers. If you get all these in one church, you could build an awesome ministry for the Kingdom of Heaven.

Pray for God to forgive you of racism. Do not teach your children what you were taught, and then watch God reverse the curse. Jesus died for every man. Should we not love all men?

Chapter Seven

SHOW THEM YOUR WOUNDS

J ohn 20:19-30 recorded the story of the resurrected Jesus showing himself to the disciples. He walked in and said, "Peace be unto you" and they did not move. He said, "Peace be unto you" and they were still discouraged. Jesus then showed them His nail-scarred hands and His pierced side, and the disciples were glad. They believed after they saw his wounds. Sometimes, you have to show people your scars. Sometimes it is in the testimony of your troubles that people will have hope to live another day. That is the purpose of this book, to show you my scars and wounds in the hope that you will avoid going where I have been or to give you hope to come out on top if you find yourself in one of these places.

I lived so wrongly for 27 long years, but in the spring of 2003, I was released from Lowndes County jail for my last time. I started going to church in Fargo,

Georgia, and I would love to be able to tell you all my problems were over at that time, but they were not. So many people quit going to church because they think their lives should be perfect from the time they enter the church. The Bible says "many are the afflictions (troubles) of the righteous."

When you get saved and start going to church, you will experience the same breakdowns and life struggles and troubles that everyone else has experienced. The Bible says that "it rains on the just and the unjust." Good people have bad days, and bad people have good days. Life is just life. Grow up and learn to make the best of it. The reason many people do not think they can live the Christian lifestyle is because they are not perfect and some preachers put out a false perception that they are perfect. These new Christians strive to be as perfect as they think the preachers to be, and they fall short. There has only ever been one perfect man that walked on earth, His name is Jesus.

Some people hear of preachers sinning or making mistakes or falling from grace, and they throw out the age-old saying, "I thought he was a man of God." If you will read the Bible, you will find that everyone named or mentioned there other than the Father, Son, and Holy Ghost made mistakes or had problems. They failed and were constantly getting into trouble.

The Apostle Paul was a murderer. King David was an adulterer. Peter denied God, cussed, and cut a man. The list of the men and women in the Bible who had problems and failures is almost endless. I am not making excuses because I had pulpit problems in the past; I am just letting you know that people make mistakes in church and out of church, preachers included.

Peter was anointed and loved by God. He told Jesus that he was ready to go to prison or even die with Him, but Jesus said, "Peter, before the rooster crows, you will deny me three times. Peter denied God, just as Jesus said, and found himself at the burn barrel with the sinners.

I have destroyed friendships with people I really loved, listening to the enemy and feeding my fleshly desires. The devil did not make me do it. It was not God's fault. It was not the pastor's fault. It takes two, but it was not the other person's fault, and the church was not to blame. I take full responsibility for the mistakes I have made. It was my place to say no to sin. The Bible says that God puts before us two paths, one to life and one to death. A couple of times in my life, I have chosen the path to death, and I have destroyed the friendships of people I really loved. I live with pain and regrets.

Every great message begins with a mess. A message is just a mess that has had time to age (mess-age). You cannot undo what has already been done. Try to forget it and move on.

I have been Peter by the burn barrel denying God. I know how it feels to be caught up in a scandal and have to quit preaching for a season. I know how it feels to break up a family. I have heard my children beg me to come home. I know how it feels to let many people down. Peter was forewarned. Jesus told him that his fall was coming. I was forewarned also. A spiritual mentor and a Grace-seasoned pastor told me what to do, but, just like Peter, I did not listen. I fell flat on my face and walked out of the hand of grace.

I felt shame, embarrassment, and hurt. I contemplated suicide all over again. People were laughing and making fun of me. They were saying "I told you so." Some people are just waiting for you to fall so that they can say "I told you so".

The only pastor with enough compassion and grace to call me and say "God loves you and will rebuild you" was a great man of God. Some called me and told me it was over for me, but the one man that probably had a right to be angry with me, called me several times through my rebuilding and made sure that I was okay. Thank you, Man of God.

I also want to thank the naysayers because many times an enemy will create a champion in you. Without Goliath, David would not have ever been a king. Without Judas, Jesus would not have had a cross and a crown.

I want to encourage the men and women of God who have fallen or may fall in the future. Get up, get up, and shake it off. People will condemn you, but God does not throw away the clay. He will remold you and use you. Some people will always remember you for the bad you have done, regardless of how much good you do. Our ministry has fed literally thousands of people. We have fed, clothed, and supplied thousands of orphans with Christmas gifts. We sow money into several charities monthly. We sow money into the Jews of Israel. God says He will bless those that bless Israel. This ministry has helped multitudes, but you can mention my name to some and they will still label me by what I used to do in my past.

You cannot live your life worrying about what somebody thinks about you. Keep living for God, and they will change their mind.

Paul was shipwrecked on the Island of Malta and the Bible says the locals had a fire built. Paul was putting sticks on the fire when a serpent came out and fastened onto his hand. Paul shook it off into the fire. Sometimes

Satan bites us, like the serpent bit Paul. I was like Paul; I got bitten while working for God. The locals said that surely God was punishing Paul. They waited for him to die. They waited for him to collapse. They expected him to lie down and not get up, but Paul kept working. He kept building a fire, and he did not die. People thought you would not rise again and that you were down for the count. The Bible says that when Paul did not die, the people changed their minds about him.

Shake it off and move on. If you do not quit on God, people will have no choice but to change their minds about you. Regardless of your past, regardless of your mistakes, God loves you. Do not use Grace as an excuse to sin, but Grace is there if you should get bitten by the enemy. God loves you and will rebuild you. Jesus was a carpenter and the spirit of the carpenter is waiting to rebuild and refurbish you. Love and pray for your enemies. They cannot stop you if you do not quit.

Scars are reminders of the pain of our past. Although I am reminded of my past, I refuse to let it stop me. You can fall forward and learn from your mistakes. Do not let failure finalize you. Falling does not make you a loser; staying down makes you a loser. Get up and move on with your life.

Chapter Eight

WHO IS FIGHTING YOUR BATTLES?

Romans 12:19: *Dearly beloved, avenge not yourselves, but rather give place unto wrath: for it is written, Vengeance is mine; I will repay, saith the Lord.*

Before I got saved, I was combative. I was a fighter. If anyone said anything about me, whether it was the truth or a lie, I was going to set the record straight. I fought my own battles, and I did not need any homeboys or a posse to do so. I did not take anything off anyone. I did not receive criticism, whether it was destructive or constructive. I avenged myself. When we fight our own battles, God sits back on the sideline and watches.

When I got saved something supernatural happened in me, and I quit fighting my own battles. I quit trying to correct the gossips. I quit calling people giving them a piece of my mind. I have had people tell lies on me, and I did not even try to correct them or fix the problem. I just gave it to God. I have had other ministries run me down, go around and talk about me, and I knew what they were saying. I just chose to let God deal with it. All my life, especially being raised in small-town USA, I witnessed people gossiping and back-biting and tale-bearing.

People that talk about others get mad when people talk about them. The Bible says that the gossiper will have their part in the lake of fire with the murderer. A three-inch tongue can kill a six-foot man. The Bible says we have the power of life and death in our tongue. When we run people down and spread rumors, whether true or not, it kills their witness, destroys their name, and breaks their spirit.

John 10:10 says: *The thief cometh not, but for to steal, and to kill, and to destroy:*

Do not let the forked tongue of Satan speak for you.

I have had people talk about my kids since I have been saved, and I just let them talk. My oldest daughter, Chelsie, was disliked by a few people, and they said she would never amount to anything. Some said she was going to go wild when she got grown. I just let them talk and prayed that God would give them peace. She was an honor student and a homecoming queen. She is a college graduate that is working in the field in which she has her degree. If I had run around and defended her, or if I had retaliated and stooped to their level and talked about them, then Chelsie's results may have been different. God can fight our battles better than we can.

In 2nd Samuel, Chapter 16, King David was approaching a town named Bahurim when a man came out of the village and cussed him. David kept riding his horse, looking straight ahead. When people talk about you, keep your eyes on God. This man kept slinging curses at David, but David did not say a word. David had a soldier riding with him that said, "If you will let me, I will go cut his head off." David told his soldier to leave the man alone.

> Proverbs 24:17-18 says: *Rejoice not when thine enemy falleth, and let not thine heart be Glad when he tumbleth: lest the Lord see it, and it displease him, and he turn away his wrath from him.*

God would have probably whipped me more if people had left me alone, but because people whipped me with their tongues, God turned His anger from me. Thank you to all of you who would not let it go.

When people talk about you, your past, your kids, or your ministry, lift your hands in surrender to God. I know it makes you mad to get laughed at, but get a divine zip of the lip and give it to God. The truth is that when we do stupid things, it gives people a chance to talk about us, a place to put their tongue.

Just like Stephen did while being stoned and Jesus did while on the cross, ask God to forgive and help the people that talk about, gossip about, and lie on you. I have already forgiven everyone that has ever said a word about me. The Bible says if we do not forgive others, we cannot be forgiven. That is found in Matthew 6:15.

Come out with your hands up, let God fight your battles, surrender to His will. Back when I was being arrested and living crazily, the cops used to say, "Come out with your hands up." My hands are up for good this time, to God. Praise Him.

Chapter Nine

WORK IT OUT

Philippians 2:12: *Wherefore, my beloved, as ye have always obeyed, not as in my presence only, but now much more in my absence, work out your own salvation with fear and trembling:*

Genesis 1:1 says: *In the beginning God created...*

The first thing scripture records is God working. God worked the first six days of Creation and rested on the seventh. This is a pattern and an example for us to follow. The Bible says a workman is worthy of his hire, and it also says in 2nd Thessalonians 3:10 "that if any should not work, neither should he eat." It is ironic that in America for the most part that the people that do not work look like they have been eating pretty well.

I am 38 years old at the time this book is being written, and I have never been unemployed or had trouble finding a job. Too many people are freeloading on unemployment and the government, applying for jobs for which they know they are not qualified, just so they can stay home and receive checks from the government. Many couples refuse to get married because government assistance will stop if they do so. Women have children, not for the love of them, but for a meal ticket and to have a dependent at tax time. Able-bodied people drain the disability system. Yet, we wonder why the government has been shut down multiple times over the past few years and why the national debt is so outrageously high.

Proverbs 21:25: *The desire of the slothful killeth him: for his hands refuse to labor.*

Proverbs 26:14*: As the door turneth upon his hinges, so doth the slothful upon his bed.*

I started working in the fields when I was around 12 or 13. I worked as farm labor until I was 16 years old. Once I turned 16, I got a job bagging groceries at Winn-Dixie, but I continued to work for farmers when I was not working at the store. When I graduated high school, I started working full time and have been working that way ever since. I came from good stock, in that respect, because my daddy started picking cotton at the age of 8. He worked until the day he died at age 66. My mama is still working at age 68. Thus, I feel I am highly qualified to talk about the importance of working to earn what you get in this world.

Whether you are starting something as simple as a diet plan or making a New Year's resolution, or something as major as starting a business or ministry, hard work, dedication, devotion, and commitment will make you successful in your endeavors. If you are determined and make up your mind that come Hell or high water you are not quitting or giving up, you will accomplish what you set out to do.

I worked for years for a man who had built a very successful, highly competitive metal fabrication business. He did not stumble into this, and it was not given to him. It took sacrifice and hard work on his part. Long after he probably no longer had to do so, he still showed up early and left late. I have noticed over my years in the work force, while watching people that he employed, that the ones who are always late and always leaving early are the same ones who constantly need money. The people who arrive early to work and stay late seem to have plenty. I have also observed over the years that some employees would get angry when business owners bought something new. They would make statements such as "There goes the Christmas bonus" and "He can afford that, but my check is so small." This is the bad attitude that keeps many people on the bottom.

I would not feel comfortable working for someone who was not wealthy. If the person who employs you does not have any money, then what hope do you have of having any? Instead of complaining about what they have, you should be thanking God for letting them get it, and asking God to keep blessing them so you will have work.

The Bible says to "rejoice with those that rejoice." Every time someone I worked for got something new, acquired more, or the company grew, I was always happy for him. Your attitude determines your altitude. If you will be happy when someone else prospers, God's hand will prosper you as well. It is the player-haters that stay on the bottom.

In all of your endeavors, from the simplicity of a diet plan to the complexity of a major business or world-changing ministry, the keys that unlock your destiny are sacrifice, dedication, devotion and commitment. Going from survival mode to being able to supply, from poverty to prosperity, is a battle that only the tough win. You have got to be tough to be successful. You have got to be willing to be talked about. You have got to stay focused and not let people sidetrack you.

In Philippians 2:12, Paul says (paraphrasing), "In my absence, work it out." It is the absence that should inspire us to want to work, the absence of money, that is. God wants you to be blessed. The absence of things you need and the things that your children need should make you want to work. Get up, get out, and go to work! If one job is not enough, then get two. You can have what you want, if you want it badly enough. It took sweat and blood, sacrifice and pain, but Jesus carried our cross to Calvary's hill and started a retirement plan that is second to none. In other words, He worked and stood strong and tough to provide for us. Now, go put your faith to work. Let us pray.

Chapter Ten

WHY I CHOSE PENTECOST

Acts 2:1-3: *And when the day of Pentecost was fully come, they were all with one accord in one place. And suddenly there came a sound from heaven as of a rushing mighty wind, and it filled all the house where they were sitting. And there appeared unto them cloven tongues like as of fire, and it sat upon each of them.*

According to the World Christian Encyclopedia, there are an estimated almost 21,000 denominations present today (David A. Barrett, Oxford University Press, 1982). Why did I choose to be a "Pentecostal" with so many from which to choose? Radical sinners need radical faith and fire to maintain a relationship with God; thus, I chose a branch of Christianity that is considered radical because

I was a very radical sinner. I will not take part in the belittling of any denomination that is a blood-bought, Jesus-believing, or Bible-teaching church. I am simply telling my story and why I chose the "denomination" that I did.

I tried going to a few different churches, from different denominations. I soon lost interest. It was as if something was missing for me. I did not know at the time what was missing. I later discovered the missing component: There was not enough zeal or passion to defeat, or even equal, the level of Hell and sinful desire that I had on me. Passive church will not change a radical culture. Some people can sit in the pew of a passive church and listen to a monotone preacher till Jesus comes back and be just fine. That is not the case with me, however.

Before I got saved and I would go out to bars and night clubs, when I would go into one that did not have much going on, I would leave. If I went to one that had a dead feeling, I left. I apply that same principle to church. If the church feels dead, I have to leave it and go somewhere that is alive with the fervor of the Holy Spirit so that I do not die.

The first time I walked into a Pentecostal church, I knew that the power of God was real and a peace overcame me because I knew that the enemy in me had to surrender to the Will of God.

In Matthew 16:13, Jesus asked the disciples: *...Whom do men say that I, the Son of man, am?*

In verse 14: *And they said Some say John the Baptist; some say Eli'jah; and others, Jeremiah, or one of the prophets.*

Verse 15: *He saith unto them, But whom say ye that I am?*

Verse 16: *And Simon Peter answered and said, Thou art the Christ, the son of the living God.*

At that moment, Peter was saved. He acknowledged Jesus as his savior. He was saved, but Jesus said in Luke 24:49: "...but tarry ye in the city of Jerusalem, until ye be endued with power from on high." Jesus was saying to Peter, "You are saved, but there is more. You are saved, but I want you baptized with the Holy Spirit.

89

I have heard people say that John was a Baptist. John baptized; he was called by what he did. John was not a member of the Baptist organization though. He was Pentecostal from the top of his head to the soles of his feet. John would have been in the Upper Room with the rest of the tongue-talkers, but he was so radical that he was killed before he could get there.

I believe there are some people from all denominations that are Bible-believing that are going to be in Heaven. You do not have to speak in tongues to go the Heaven. You do not have to be Pentecostal to go to Heaven. I just choose to live in the fire. Pentecost had what I needed to overcome my demons.

In Acts 19:2, Paul meets a group of disciples. They had to be saved to be disciples. He said, "Have you received the Holy Ghost since you believed?" And they said, "We have not heard of the Holy Ghost." The Bible says that Paul laid his hands on them and they received the Holy Ghost and spoke in tongues.

Some people are stumped by the scripture in 1st Corinthians 13:8 that says that "tongues will cease." Some teach a lie that the tongues, miracles, signs and wonders stopped with the disciples of the Bible, but the devil is a liar. The book of Acts does not end with amen. We are still living it. We serve a God too great to have been stopped for 2,000 years. I do not know about you, but I speak in tongues and I prophesy and see the fruits of it in my life. A three-time felon, South Georgia hell-raiser becoming a preacher is enough proof for me.

Tongues will cease one day. When we are in Heaven, there will be no need for tongues and interpretations. We will all speak Hebrew, according to the Book of Revelation.

Acts 1:8 tells us that the Holy Spirit gives us power to live holy lives and power to witness. The Bible says in John 16:14 that He is for all believers, so they can receive with power certain gifts. Lamentations 1:3 says that "Judah (and Judah always means *praise*) has gone into captivity." Some churches have gone into captivity and have lost their praise. I refuse to be a part of a church that does not praise God. I am an aisle-running, pew-jumping, hand-raising, top of my voice shouting, cut my spiritual teeth in the fire of Pentecost, and the smoke will not do, praiser.

If you have been in church for years and you are still struggling with something in your life, do not stay somewhere because it was your grandmother's church, go somewhere and get in the fire and feel the power of God. When you get saved, the Holy Ghost is with you. He lays it on your heart to pray, He comforts you, He convicts you of sin, and He leads you to church on Sunday and meets you at the altar.

The Bible says that Jesus was given the Spirit without measure. There are different measures of the Spirit for believers. There is a baptism of the Spirit, an in-filling of His presence and the evidence is speaking in tongues; and it is for you.

Chapter Eleven

THE CHALLENGE
OF CHANGE

Genesis 35:2: *Then Jacob said unto his household, and to all that were with him, Put away the strange gods that are among you, and be clean, and change your garments:*

O n your journey through life one of the hardest things you will ever do is change. We are creatures of habit and routine. My greatest enemy has always been within me. I am my own worst critic. I am my worst enemy, and the hardest thing I have ever had to do was change.

In Exodus, chapter 4, the Bible says that God told Moses He was going to send him to Pharaoh to show wonders in Egypt. It also says that Moses started going to Egypt when God confronted him and was about to kill him. Wait a minute! God just told

Moses that he was going to bless him, and now he plans to kill him? What is up with that? The Bible does not record Moses doing anything wrong. Get this: Moses had not circumcised his son. He had not made the proper changes that God required. Something as small and simple as the circumcision of a child kept two million people in bondage and held back a mega-ministry. You can make a change in the right place and turn your life around. There are things in your life today that God will not let go into your tomorrow.

It was a private place that got Moses in trouble, his refusal to change the private place. The Bible says that "He dwells in the secret place (private place) and shall abide under the shadow of the Almighty." If you neglect prayer, you will surely spiritually die.

The Bible records that Zipporah, Moses' wife, took a stone and circumcised the child. She did not take a razor, but a stone. Sometimes in life you do not always have what you want, but God will always give you what you need. Zipporah circumcised the child and threw the foreskin at Moses' feet. Zipporah made a sacrifice and threw it at the father's feet and saved his life. Many people would have been hurled out into eternity if someone had not prayed and made the sacrifice of praise and fell at Father God's feet on their behalf.

I can empathize with Moses; change is challenging. I did not change overnight. Change is hard, and it takes a fighter to do it. Hank Williams Jr. said a mouthful when he said in his song that "old habits are hard to break." I had to change the way I talked and the way I thought. I am still working on that latter one. I had to change in that I could no longer cuss someone out. I had to change the way I coped with problems, learning to trust God to help deal with them. It took time to learn to pray instead of resorting to nicotine and alcohol to settle my nerves and ease my tension. It took time to learn to control and change my temper. It also took time to change the fact that I did not respect others; it took time to train myself to say "sir" and "ma'am" and to change an unpleasant attitude to one that would honor God. It took time to learn to not look at a woman as free game, and it took time to learn to love my enemies when I had spent so much time punching them in the face. It took time to learn patience when I got my way for so long. It hurts to wait on a home-cooked meal when you have eaten fast food for so long. It took lots of time to change all the negative parts of me.

The religious people will not like this, but that is okay. If you are struggling with a problem, do not give up on God. Do not give up on yourself or church. Keep coming. You will begin to get better. It took 27 years to make the mess I had made of myself, and it took time to mend and heal and change that mess into something wonderful and positive. It is challenging, but like Moses and just like me, you can do it. Grace and Mercy are on your side and the power of the cross will change you. A few changes in the right place will make a big difference in your life. Do not listen to the religious, traditional church folk and do not give up on yourself. Attend church, pray for wisdom, and let God help you make the alterations necessary to live better the second half of your life.

God told Jacob to change his garments. You can change your outlook, and you can change the way others see you. A few changes in the right place will change the way that people view you. Let us pray for change. Real change will not start at the White House; it will start at your house, at an altar. An altar will alter (change) your life. I am praying for our change.

Chapter Twelve

GIVE SO YOU CAN LIVE

Genesis 8:22: *While the earth remaineth, seedtime and harvest, and cold and heat, and summer and winter, and day and night shall not cease.*

F armers understand the concept portrayed in this scripture best. To have a harvest, you have to sow a seed. There is a sad fact alive today: poverty has been here from the beginning, and it will be here when Jesus comes back. Poverty is a spirit, and it is not prejudiced. It will affect all that will buy into it.

Some children go to bed hungry right here in the richest nation on earth, and some children start school in raggedy hand-me-down clothes. Some children are picked on because of the vehicle their parents drive and use to drop them off at school. As the school bus pulls up to a run-down house, the children get off the bus in shame and embarrassment. Poverty is real, and it is depressing.

Poverty is a generational curse. Do not cry just yet though. God has a remedy for poverty. God is ready for somebody to break the cycle of poverty. Every generation should not have to start out on the bottom, fighting their way to the top. We have all seen it, instances where granddaddy did not have anything, daddy started out with nothing, and we were born with nothing. Our children should not have to fight as hard as we did. It is God's Will to prosper you in a way that you will be able to leave an inheritance for your children and grandchildren.

When I got saved, I was working as a welder/millwright. We were working shutdowns out of town. I was making good money. I would bring home up to $1,500 a week and more, depending on the hours. When I got saved, I knew I could not keep working out of town because I needed all the church I could get. The motels, the alcohol, the bars and clubs, the women, the prostitutes, and the pressure was too much for a new Christian. When I quit going out of town, I took a drastic pay cut. I went from more than enough to poverty.

I was not born rich by any means. My mama worked two jobs many times to give me what I had. I knew what it was to struggle. I knew what the bottom looked like. There is an old country song that says, "If the devil danced in empty pockets, he'd have a ball in mine." My pockets have been the devil's dance floor many times. (Take a laugh break here because you have to laugh sometimes to keep from crying.)

> Psalms 119:32 says: *I will run the way of thy commandments, when thou shalt enlarge my heart.*

When I got saved, God enlarged my heart. He gave me a giver's heart. I read in the Bible that "whatsoever a man soweth, that shall he also reap." I read that if you give, God will give it back, "pressed down, shaken together, and over-flowing." I read that if you give to the poor, you are lending money to God.

I bought into the principle that I had to give to live. I had to sow to grow. I was broke, and I would count change and go to the store and buy a two dollar and fifty cent money order and send it to an orphanage to feed hungry kids. The store owners looked at me like I was crazy, but I did not care. I would send Barbie dolls and little trucks to children's orphanages at Christmas. I would take the leftovers from my mama's Thanksgiving dinner and ride around town, giving it to hungry people. I had a heart to give, thanks to my Heavenly Father.

When I paid tithes, I did not pay bills first and give God what was left. I paid God His 10 percent first, and then dealt with the rest. I have given my way out of poverty. I graduated from the two and a half dollar club because when I started giving to God's people, God started giving to me. He will do the same for you. I have given away gold rings, expensive horses too. I picked up a homeless man walking down the road, and, at the time, I had a gold ring on that my daddy gave to me. The homeless man told me he had never had anything nice in his whole life. He was not a panhandler. I knew this man, and I knew his story. When I dropped him off at the pile of rubble in which he was living, just a lean-to under some trees, I gave him that ring.

I have pulled through fast food lanes and bought me a meal, and when I got to the intersection, I would hand it to somebody with a "will work for food" sign. I have sent money to people that have run me down, and I did not even let them know from where it came. I have bought groceries for people when I needed some myself. I have had men tell me they liked the shirt I was wearing, and the next time I saw them I gave it to them, washed and ironed.

Everybody will not understand this. The Bible says that carnal-minded people will not understand spiritual things. I do not do all of this giving to receive any glory for myself, but to glorify God within me. I gave myself right out of the hand of poverty. The love of God inspired me to give to others, expecting nothing in return, and God prospered me for being faithful in my giving to others.

So many people are afraid to give. Others would give, but do not do so because they wonder what the recipient will do with the money. "Will he buy drugs or alcohol?" they wonder. If you give your money to a man that says he is homeless or hungry, God is going to bless you for your heart and your spirit to give, and He will hold the man responsible for what he does with the money. So, feel free to give as God lays on your heart to do so.

I know people who pay their tithes, but they want to know where every dime goes. When I give my money, I release it. Do not let that Judas spirit control you. Judas betrayed Jesus for thirty pieces of silver. He was greedy, and we all know what that greed got him.

I now understand from where Jesus was coming in Acts 20:35 when he said "It is better to give than receive." I am a giver because of His love within

101

me. I give blood to the Red Cross. I sow money into orphans, widows, rehab centers, and television ministries. Any time there is a natural disaster, I sow money into the rebuilding. You can give your way out of poverty. You can give your time as a volunteer, and you can give your talent by sharing it with others for free.

Rich people throw crumbs and pennies at beggars and call that giving to appease their consciences. Some will see someone in need and turn around, or will change sides of the street, to avoid them, ignoring the voice of God telling them to give. We are to be the hands and feet of God. That means walking toward the needy and giving. Understand that God will give you wisdom with this: when to give, how much to give, and to whom to give. I am not going to give money to a drug abuser or an alcoholic; instead, I will buy him a meal or a bottle of water or get him a motel room for the night to get him out of a storm. I am not going to support his habit, but I will still show him the love for him that God has given to me.

Proverbs 19:17 says: *He that hath pity upon the poor lendeth unto the Lord; and that which he hath given will he pay him again.*

You can give your way out of poverty. I cannot say this enough. The best investment you will ever make is giving your money to God. God's checks do not bounce. God is never late on a payment, and Heaven does not need a bailout. The sky is the limit with God; there is no debt ceiling. God walks on streets of gold.

Givers do not depend on the economy. King David said, "I was once young, but now I am old. I have never seen the righteous forsaken or their seed begging bread."

For security and confidence, people have asked me to remain quiet. I cannot tell you all that God, through His people, has done for me, but please take my word for it. You cannot out-give God. If you will become a giver, God will take you from getting what you can to getting what you want. Pray for God to enlarge your heart. I give because of my love for people. I do not give just to get back more, but because I give, He does give me back more. God wants you to be blessed; the more you have the more you can give. Let us pray.

Chapter Thirteen

REINSTATED

Joel 2:25-26: *And I will restore to you the years that the locust hath eaten, the cankerworm, and the caterpillar, and the palmerworm, my great army which I sent among you. And you shall eat plenty and be satisfied...*

Many times in life, trouble and tragedy will strip you like a plague of locusts in a farmer's field, leaving you standing in a barren field of dreams. I have had three felonies, all of which were due to violence, and many misdemeanors. When I got my first felony, and left the courtroom, I was told to report to my probation officer.

At court, I was given a sheet of paper full of all the *Cannots*. You *cannot* vote. You *cannot* drink alcohol. You *cannot* have a firearm. You *cannot* be

within a hundred yards of the victim. You *cannot*;
you *cannot*....

I reported to the probation officer, and he gave
me a list of *Could Nots*. I *could not* be out past 7:00
p.m. I *could not* go out of town. I *could not* leave the
house before 7:00 a.m.

Over the course of eight years, I learned to hate
the words *cannot* and *could not*. I appeared to be free,
but I was still bound. I was not physically behind bars,
but I was mentally locked up. I lost all of my rights,
even though I was born a free American; ignorant
decisions that I had made had stripped me of those
rights. Deemed "dangerous" to society, I was not
even trusted, by my own country, to cast a rational
vote. I was in my mid 20's, and I was being told what
and what not to do, when and where not to come
and go. I am not alone. Many people are stripped of
their dignity, like a field destroyed by caterpillars and
worms, left with no hope, no plans, no future, and all
that is left is shame, regret, and the pain of a past and
the past mistakes that cannot be changed.

Elections came and went, and I was not allowed to
vote. Hunting seasons passed, and I was not allowed
to take my children hunting. The Bible says that
Jesus learned obedience from the things He suffered.
I learned to obey the law from the things I suffered.

Regardless of the case or charge, people and government cannot hold down what God has set free. I got saved in jail, but I still had all those charges, fines, and fees. I still had probation. My soul was free, but I still had to harvest the bad seeds that I had sown. The last time I was released from jail, I had twenty thousand dollars of hospital bills and restitution to pay. I know a little bit about paying a debt to society and the time it takes to win back trust.

I have good news: When God is on your side, nobody can stop you. For safety and security, I cannot mention names, but I had prayed and prayed for God to let me get my gun rights back and to be able to vote again. When you ask Jesus in your heart and pray, He hears. God allowed me to meet a man that had friends in the right high places. He spoke up for me, and the paperwork (his positive words about me) was taken to the right person. Within 48 hours, my charges were wiped away. I had a clean slate. I voted in the last election. I went hunting last year. For the first time in years, I had a clean record, in my heart and within the state system. God is good.

In John 18:30, the Jews called Jesus a malefactor (which means felon). Of course, he was lied about. He never sinned; he was falsely charged as a felon. He died on a death bed called the cross and was put in a grave, with a stone blocking the door. However, God brought Him out. He arose with all power.

Regardless of your case or your history, regardless of the restrictions that have been placed upon you, if you serve God, He will turn it around. Jesus was innocent and perfect, and He was falsely accused. I was found guilty, and I got what I deserved. I paid my debt. I did my time. I did not complain or try to get out of it. I actually deserved more punishment than I got. I plead guilty to the State of Georgia and to God. Now, though, I am free...free indeed.

Whatever is holding you back cannot hold you forever. The grave had to turn Lazarus loose when the Lord spoke. Call on God and let Him handle your case. What He did for me, He will do for you. I am reinstated, and you can be too. The prophet Joel said, (put simply) "God will restore (reinstate) what has been destroyed."

Let us pray for restoration.

Chapter Fourteen

THE FINAL WORD

Matthew 28:18-20: *And Jesus came and spake unto them, saying, All power is given unto me in heaven and in earth. Go ye therefore, and teach all the nations, baptizing them in the name of the Father, and the Son, and the Holy Ghost: teaching them to observe all things whatsoever I have commanded you: and, lo, I am with you alway, even unto the end of the world. Amen.*

These were Jesus' closing remarks in Matthew. As I close and this book ends, life goes on. My closing remarks to you are these: Life is hard, and sometimes it is not fair, but it is worth living. Every day is a new day of Grace and a chance to start over. Live your life to the fullest, and do not ever give up on your dreams. Do not let hope fade and your vision and destiny die. Love and forgive your enemies. Do not give up on your family. Always remember that people make mistakes, and just as God forgives us, so should we forgive them for their mistakes. Do not let hard times and troubles make you bitter; you look so much better wearing a smile than you do wearing a frown. Work hard, but allow time for play and rest. Live every day like it is your last because it very well may be. Do not go to bed angry, and learn to start every morning thanking God for another day.

God has great plans for your life. Find a good church that is on fire, a Bible-teaching, Jesus-believing, people-loving church, and be faithful and dedicated to it. Jesus came and built the church and then died for it so we could have power. The least we can do is live for Him.

For three years now, I've been pastoring a growing, successful church that has helped thousands of people locally, nationally, and overseas. There is nothing too hard for God. He took a down-and-out felon, an adulterous alcoholic, a barroom brawler, a superstitious, self-centered wreck and changed him (me) into that pastor of that growing church. I was addicted to nicotine, lust, anger and rage, and the list goes on of my faults and failures. Satan thought he had me, but God had better plans for me. Who would have ever thought that God would have taken a man as messed up as I was and make a way for me to help on mission trips in Alaska and Hawaii, and help conduct a communion supper in Israel. As bad as I have been, and as many mistakes as I have made, He now trusts me to lead a flock of His precious people. God is good.

If God has done all that for me, just imagine what He could do for you. Give God a chance and let Him make all things new. There is a champion inside you. There is a dream alive in you, and I know you love God.

Would you please pray this prayer of salvation with me?

> *Father, I come to you as I am, a sinner. I have sinned against you and Heaven. Please forgive me. Come into my heart and save my soul. I know Jesus died for my sins, died on a cross, rose the third day, ascended to Heaven, and is sitting on your right side, soon to return. I accept Jesus as my Savior and I turn my life over to you; in Jesus' name. Amen.*

If you have confessed that and believe it in your heart, then you are saved. Your name is written in the Lamb's Book of Life and angels are rejoicing. I am proud of you, and God loves you. Share your decision with someone and find a home church soon so that you can worship God with others like you.

> John 3:16: *For God so loved the world, that he gave his only begotten so, that whosoever believeth on him should not perish, but have everlasting life.*

I will see you in Heaven.

CPSIA information can be obtained at www.ICGtesting.com
Printed in the USA
LVOW05s0748150114

369404LV00002B/2/P